THE
1930s

Richard Tames

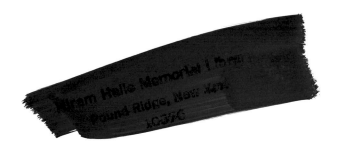

Franklin Watts
New York · London · Toronto · Sydney

© 1991 Franklin Watts

Franklin Watts, Inc.
387 Park Avenue South
New York, N.Y. 10016

Library of Congress Cataloging-in-Publication Data
Tames, Richard.
    The 1930s/Richard Tames.
        p.   cm.—(Picture history of the 20th century)
    Summary: Text and pictures highlight the main events of the 1930s.
    ISBN 0-531-14059-8
    1. Europe—History—1918-1945—Pictorial works—Juvenile
literature. 2. Great Britain—History—George V, 1910-1936—
Pictorial works—Juvenile literature. 3. Great Britain—History—
George VI, 1936-1952—Pictorial works—Juvenile literature.
4. World War, 1939-1945—Causes—Pictorial works—Juvenile
literature.   [1. History. Modern—20th century.]   I. Title.
II. Series
D725.T35   1991
940.5′2—dc20   90-32322 CIP AC

Design: K and Co
Editor: Hazel Poole
Picture Research: Sarah Ridley
Printed in Belgium

Photographs: Norman Barrett 38(BOTH), 39(BR); BFI Stills, Posters and Designs
26(B), 27(T), 28(BL), 28(BR), 29(TL); Bettmann Archive 20(T); Gunn Brinson
9(BL), 43(T); Brown Brothers 21(BR), 24(B), 37(BL), 43(B); courtesy of Martha Dix,
Immenhofer/Bodensee, Germany 37(BR); Mary Evans Picture Library 7(BL), 8(T),
9(BR), 10(B), 11(C), 13(BL), 18(T), 23(C), 25(TL), 26(T), 27(BL), 28(T), 30(T),
33(BR), 34(BOTH), 35(T), 35(BR), 40(BOTH), 41(ALL); Mary Evans/Explorer 12(T);
with thanks to Hoover plc 36(B); Hulton-Deutsch 10(T), 17(BL), 19(B), 45(BC);
Kobal Collection 29(B), 30(B), 33(T), 33(C); courtesy of the London Transport
Museum 37(T); Robert Opie 21(TL), 21(TR), 24(T), 35(BL), 42(T); with thanks to
Penguin Books Ltd 32(T); Photofest 33(BL), 42(B); Popperfoto 6(BOTH), 7(TL),
7(BL), 7(BR), 8(B), 9(T), 11(B), 12(B), 13(BR), 14(BOTH), 15(BOTH), 16(B), 19(T),
19(C), 20(B), 25(TR), 25(BR), 27(BR), 31(T), 31(BR), 32(B), 39(BL), 44(ALL),
45(BL), 45(BR); Retrograph Archive Collection 29(TR), 31(BL), 43(C); The Herman
Seid Collection 39(T); Topham 7(BR), 11(T), 13(T), 16(T), 17(T), 18(B), 23(B),
24(BL); UPI/Bettmann 21(BL), 22(B), 23(T); courtesy of the Board of Trustees of the
V & A Museum 36(T).

cover: BFI Stills, Posters and Designs/Mary Evans Picture Library/Popperfoto
frontispiece: Mary Evans Picture Library

CONTENTS

Introduction

The 1930s were a decade of challenge and change. The Great Depression caused world trade to collapse and created economic disruption in many nations. Businesses shut down, production halted, and millions of people found themselves unemployed.

The fragile European status quo gradually disintegrated. Communists and Fascists clashed when each backed opposing sides in the Spanish Civil War. Throughout the thirties, the disarmed and economically unstable Western European democracies sought to preserve the peace. Faced with Fascist demands for boundary changes, they adopted a policy of appeasement, making territorial concessions at international conferences. In the absence of resistance, the Fascists simply increased their demands and annexed countries. Meanwhile Japan began a full-scale invasion of China. At the end of the decade, the Soviet Union and Germany patched up their differences over Spain and signed a nonaggression pact, leaving them free to prey on neighboring states. With Germany's invasion of Poland, the specter of a second world war became a reality.

Faced with unsettling events in Europe and Asia, the government of the United States adopted an isolationist position. The American people refused to become involved in other people's wars and attended to their own economic recovery. Those who had jobs could enjoy the benefits of technological advances. Cheap electricity made possible many labor-saving appliances in their homes. Sound and technicolor were introduced into movie theaters. Housing, food, and transportation became less expensive. At the end of the decade, while others fought, Americans celebrated their progress at a World's Fair.

The United States in the 1930s

The worldwide trade slump of 1929–31 plunged the United States into a depression which, made worse by a drought, severely tested faith in "the American Dream."

By 1930, over four million people were out of work and this number had doubled at the end of 1931.

An increase in crime in cities and impoverishment in the country added to an unfamiliar sense of insecurity.

America no longer seemed to know where it was going.

Fortunately, President Franklin Delano Roosevelt did – or at least he appeared to. Reassuring his fellow Americans "that the only thing we have to fear is fear itself," he organized many programs for creating new jobs and giving people confidence in the future. Historians disagree about how far this "New Deal" really did contribute to economic recovery. But few doubt that "FDR" inaugurated a new style of politics using power actively to promote public welfare.

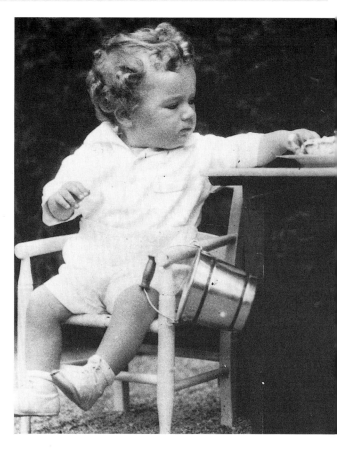

△ The 1932 kidnapping of aviator Charles Lindbergh's infant son shocked America. Despite the payment of a $50,000 ransom, the child was found dead 73 days later. The murderer, a German immigrant, was tried and executed in 1936.

◁ This Chicago soup kitchen was supported by notorious gangster Al Capone. In a land of legendary plenty, millions of Americans were reduced to the edge of starvation.

◁ President Roosevelt used the radio to appeal directly to the American people through his famous "fireside chats."

▽ Bank robber, jail-breaker and murderer John Dillinger was tracked down by the FBI and shot in 1934.

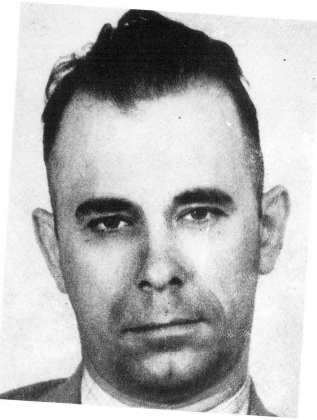

◁ Boulder Dam, Colorado, one of many dams built to provide jobs, electricity and flood control.

▽ A Texas farm overwhelmed by dust storms following the terrible 1935 drought.

Stalin's Russia

Joseph Stalin (translated as steel) was a totalitarian dictator determined to bring all aspects of Soviet life under his control. He set the Soviet Union on a path of forced modernization through a series of "Five Year Plans" to create a highly centralized economy.

Priority was given to heavy industrial projects and the collectivization of agriculture at the expense of living standards. These frantic efforts evoked much heroic idealism and even more brutal exploitation. Peasants who resisted the forcible takeover of their lands were liquidated either by mass murder or by deliberately caused famines.

To strengthen his hold on power even further, Stalin began a series of "purges" from 1935 onwards which were to lead to the murder of thousands of loyal and bewildered Communist party members and senior army officers. He transformed the Communist party into a "monolithic" organization, intolerant of dissent and willing to obey him. Yet, throughout the 1930s, Western admirers hailed the Soviet Union as a workers' paradise.

△ An Italian magazine of 1938 shows OGPU troops (secret police) about to bayonet an alleged Trotskyist sympathizer. Left-wingers dismissed this as Fascist counter-propaganda.

◁ The Moscow underground – a showpiece to dazzle foreign visitors who were carefully shielded from the harsh realities of state exploitation and terrorism.

◁ The tractor was a potent symbol of determination to overcome the traditional backwardness of Russian farming. But it was control of the land that mattered.

▽ Stalin developed a cult of personality that portrayed him as a universal genius – not merely a political leader but a poet and philosopher as well.

▽ A 1932 propaganda poster depicts members of the Communist youth movement – well-dressed, well-fed and cheerfully determined to defend the revolution. Art, like every other activity, was pressed into the service of political power.

Hitler's Germany

National Socialist (Nazi) party leader Adolf Hitler became Chancellor of Germany in January 1933. Within a month, the burning of the Reichstag (legislature) had given him the excuse to extend his powers to rule by emergency decree. He began a process of "Gleichschaltung" (streamlining) which eliminated potential sources of opposition and made Germany into a one-party dictatorship. He also undertook a vigorous program of public works and rearmament which bolstered national pride and dramatically reduced unemployment. Hitler believed that Germans were the descendants of an Aryan "master race" who deserved to rule the world. To him, Slavs and gypsies were useful only as slaves. Rabidly anti-semitic, Hitler initiated a program which led to the persecution of German Jews. Determined to fulfill the Nazi dream of "Ein Reich, Ein Volk, Ein Fuhrer" (One State, One People, One Leader), he annexed territories with German populations. Hitler then set about the forceful creation of a "New Order in Europe" by invading Poland in September 1939.

△ In May 1938, Hitler opened a factory to mass-produce Ferdinand Porsche's Volkswagen ("People's Car"). However, few cars ever found their way into the hands of German workers although many joined programs to save for one.

◁ The destruction of the German Reichstag was blamed on a deranged Dutch communist, Marinus van der Lubbe. The new Nazi government moved very swiftly when it came to rounding up suspects and opponents.

◁ Nazi party members burn "un-German" books in May 1933. Hitler believed that he had a mission to purge Germany of any alien and, in particular, Jewish cultural influences.

△ Hitler reviews a parade of Brownshirts, the Nazi militia, on a "Party Day" in the medieval city of Nuremberg, a favorite location for spectacular rallies.

◁ A shop in the port of Danzig/Gdansk sells Julius Streicher's racist newspaper and displays a poster saying "The Jews are our misfortune."

Spain's agony

In 1931, King Alfonso XIII abdicated and Spain was declared a republic. Despite regional unrest, the new republican government undertook many needed reforms. However, in 1933, a conservative government undid these reforms and crushed the workers' uprisings. In February 1936, a left-wing coalition was formed that consisted of Republicans, Socialists and Communists and became known as the Popular Front.

In July, General Francisco Franco airlifted army units from Morocco to the Spanish mainland to challenge the Popular Front government. In the Civil War that followed, Germany and Italy supported Franco with men and weapons, while Russia and Mexico aided the government, as did an "International Brigade" of idealistic volunteers.

Barcelona finally fell to the rebels in January 1939 and Madrid in March, after a siege of 28 months. The war cost perhaps as many as half a million lives, divided Europe like no other single issue and set the Spanish economy back a quarter of a century.

▽ Government troops, mostly without uniforms, cluster behind a makeshift barricade to fire on rebel troops besieged in the

Alcazar (citadel) of Toledo in July 1936. Despite artillery bombardment, the rebels held out until they were relieved.

△ Francisco Bahamonde Franco was a career soldier and a firm believer in Spain's Catholic and aristocratic traditions.

Personally austere in lifestyle, he ruled Spain from the time of his victory until his death in 1975.

◁ Dolores Ibarruri (La Pasionaria) was a brilliant public speaker who, during the Spanish Civil War, personified the defiant spirit of the republic and its slogan "No Pasaran!" ("They shall not pass!"). A lifelong Communist, she then spent over 40 years in exile but later returned to Spain and politics.

▽ On April 26, 1937, German planes of the Condor Legion destroyed the ancient Basque city of Guernica in a matter of hours, killing some 3,000 civilians. Horrified Europeans saw it as a glimpse of what a second world war would bring. Exiled Spanish artist Pablo Picasso made it his masterpiece.

▽ A left-wing propaganda poster shows a death-bearing Nazi volunteer with the slogan "How the Church has sown religion in Spain."

The challenge of Fascism

Fascism originated in Italy and the Mussolini regime set the style for would-be imitators throughout Europe. Fascist movements had certain common features – rabid anticommunism, contempt for parliaments and civil liberties and a belief in the political virtues of violence. Fascist leaders tended to present themselves to the world as men of destiny who would lead devoted followers towards a glorious future.

By the 1930s, there were active Fascist groups in almost every European country. Left-wing opponents of Fascism, such as the British writer George Orwell, feared that it was acquiring the character of an international movement. Yet Fascism was in its nature intensely nationalistic and each group differed from each other in its aims and characteristics. The racist element which was so pronounced in Germany and much of Eastern Europe was seen to be largely lacking in Italy and Spain. Whatever its nature, however, Fascism made the most headway wherever democracy was unwilling to confront it.

△ Sir Oswald Mosley accepts the salutes of "Blackshirts," members of the British Union of Fascists at a Rally held at the Albert Hall.

◁ Dr. Engelbert Dollfuss, Chancellor of Austria, proclaiming a new Fascist-style constitution in May 1934. Two months later he was assassinated by Nazis wanting union with Germany.

◁ Mussolini consciously used settings and symbols of Roman glory to stimulate support for re-creating an overseas empire in Africa and a militaristic state at home. He also secretly subsidized imitators like Degrelle and Mosley.

▷ Leon Degrelle, failed lawyer and leader of the Belgian Rexists. Fiery speeches, appealing to emotion rather than reason, were the trademark of Fascist leaders.

Turmoil in Asia

Throughout the 1930s the stability of Asia was threatened by struggles for independence and the emerging conflict between its two most important sovereign states.

China was divided between supporters of General Chiang Kai-Shek's Kuomintang government and those who favored communism led by Mao Tse Tung. In 1931, Japanese troops seized the Chinese-owned state of Manchuria and in its place set up its own state of Manchukuo. This action brought about international condemnation and Japan consequently withdrew from the League of Nations.

In 1937, Japan launched a full-scale invasion of the rest of China which resulted in Communist and Nationalist forces finally joining together in an attempt to defy Japanese troops.

Meanwhile, in India, Mahatma Gandhi tried to expel the British using nonviolent and disciplined mass-action. The British responded with police crackdowns and constitutional reforms.

▽ In 1930, Mahatma "Great Souled" Gandhi organized a challenge to the government's salt monopoly.

△ Pu Yi, last survivor of China's last dynasty, was used by Japan as emperor of their puppet state of Manchukuo.

◁ General Chiang Kai-Shek, a professional soldier and head of the Chinese Nationalist (Kuomintang) government, spent most of the decade fighting the Communists and trying to promote a neo-Confucian revival.

▽ Mao Tse Tung's 6,000 mile Long March (1934) took the Communists to safety in remote Yenan, but less than one-third of his 100,000 followers survived the ordeal. The Japanese invasion in 1937 (below left) forced Mao and Nationalist rival Chiang Kai-Shek into an uneasy alliance of resistance.

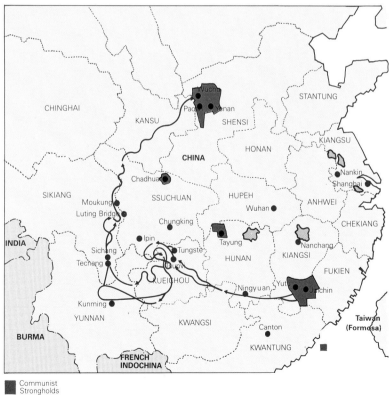

■ Communist Strongholds

The road to war

During the early 1930s, as a result of previous peace settlements, Germany was reduced to a shrunken, demilitarized state while Italy was a small, insignificant country. Both Hitler and Mussolini had grandiose dreams of restoring their nations to former glory. Determined to make Italy into a "Third Rome," Mussolini completed his conquest of Ethiopia in 1936. In 1939, he invaded Albania. To transform Germany into a "Third Reich," Hitler rearmed his nation and reclaimed the Rhineland in 1936. The two leaders also signed an alliance forming the Rome-Berlin Axis. By the end of 1938, Hitler had annexed Austria and dismembered Czechoslovakia by taking over the Sudetenland. After signing a nonaggression pact with Stalin in 1939, he invaded Poland.

The Western European democracies, ill-prepared for war, reluctantly conceded that perhaps Germany had been ill-treated and Italy short-changed. As a result, the Western leaders chose to appease the dictators by accepting their acquisitions and conquests. Only when Hitler posed a threat to Poland did they realize that their own security was endangered and prepared to use force.

△ Amiable Austria tempts a reborn Germany, symbolized by the hi-tech plane used by Austrian-born Adolf Hitler in his 1932 election campaign. The Anschluss (union with Germany) came in March 1938 and was overwhelmingly endorsed by the whole nation.

◁ German forces escort Polish prisoners during the invasion of September 1939. Despite gallant resistance, Polish forces were crushed in three weeks by the Blitzkrieg tactics of German mechanized warfare supported by superior air power.

◁ September 30, 1938 –
British Prime Minister
Neville Chamberlain
returns from crisis talks in
Munich to reassure
cheering Londoners, "I
believe it is peace for our
time." The price was a
German takeover of
Czechoslovakia.

▽ The plane that became
a legend, the Spitfire, tests
its eight Browning
machine guns which could
fire 1,260 rounds a
minute. Faster and more
maneuverable than the
German ME 109, the
"Spit" represented
Britain's commitment to a
strong air defense.

◁ German troops are
welcomed as liberators by
the German-speaking
minority living in
Czechoslovakia's
Sudetenland border areas
in October 1938.

Transportation

Throughout the decade, increasing car ownership brought the convenience of private motoring to millions, but it was aviation that consistently captured the imagination as every year brought new headlines.

In 1930, Amy Johnson became the first woman to fly solo from England to Australia in 17 days. In 1932, Amelia Earhart became the first woman to fly solo across the Atlantic in 15 hours 18 minutes.

Nineteen thirty-three saw a world record for nonstop distance flying of 8,531 km (5,301 mi), the first flight over Everest and the first around the world solo flight. In 1936, a world altitude record of 15,250 m (50,033 ft) was established. Regular airline services were also extended. Pan-American Airways inaugurated a trans-Pacific service in 1935 and a trans-Atlantic service in 1939. It was passenger liners, however, that still carried most people across the oceans, and the launching of the luxurious liners *Queen Mary* and its French rival the *Normandie* showed that air travel was still seen by the masses as an adventure.

(Above right) Amelia Earhart, the first aviatrix to fly the Atlantic solo.

▷ **In May 1937, the German airship *Hindenburg* exploded trying to moor at Lakehurst, New Jersey, with the loss of 36 lives. In 1930, 48 people died when the British airship R101 crashed at Beauvais near Paris.**

IMPERIAL AIRWAYS

G-AAGX

DAILY DEPARTURES from AIRWAY TERMINUS
SEPTEMBER 1931

07.15	Sundays Only	PARIS
07.15	Weekdays Only	PARIS, B
07.15	Saturdays Only	FRANCE
		GREECE
		IRAQ, P'
		SUDAN
		TANGA

◁ By 1932, Imperial Airways had begun an airmail service to South Africa and introduced a passenger service to Singapore in 1933. In 1935, a flight from London to Australia, took $12\frac{1}{2}$ days – more than three times as fast as by sea.

★ The same experience which produced the fuel for Sir Malcolm Campbell, and the same red Ethyl fluid, go into the blending of the Esso Ethyl petrol you buy from the roadside pumps.

301 MILES AN HOUR ON SPECIAL ESSO Ethyl !

It is typical of SIR MALCOLM CAMPBELL'S thoroughness that he had his own supplies of special Esso Ethyl shipped from England to Utah –6,000 miles–for this magnificent achievement.

ESSO ETHYL

▷ Sir Malcolm Campbell set the world land speed record of 500 kph (311 mph) in 1935 and the world water speed record of 288 kph (179 mph) in 1939. As a racing driver, he won over 400 trophies.

▽ By 1936, 160,000 trailers (mobile homes), traveled U.S. roads, combining affordable housing with cheap transportation.

△ In July 1938, Douglas G. Corrigan set off from New York on a flight to California. He landed in Dublin, Ireland instead, becoming a celebrity and earning the nickname "Wrong Way Corrigan."

Science and technology

Throughout the 1930s, the United States maintained its position as a leader in both pure science and the application of technology to the improvement of everyday life.

In February 1930, astronomer Clyde Tombaugh discovered a new planet beyond Neptune, on the edge of the solar system. It was decided to call it Pluto.

In 1932, Karl Jansky of Bell Laboratories detected radio-wave emissions from stars, thus laying the foundations of a new science – radio astronomy.

The year 1930 saw Massachusetts grocers offer a new convenience food – frozen peas. Frozen meat and fish had been known for some years, but it had not been possible to treat vegetables in the same way until Clarence J. Birdseye discovered that "quick-freezing" preserved freshness without destroying texture and taste.

In the same year, Wallace Carrothers, a chemist at the Du Pont company, invented a new artificial fiber to be known as nylon. Its first use was for women's stockings.

Erinoid Toilet Brush Set

1 Silk Pink (Light) 2 Amber 3 Dark Red 4 Silk Pink (Dark) 5 Greenstone
6 Silver 7 Bronze 8 Dark Blue 9 Light Red

These beautiful Brush Sets, which are exceptionally light in weight, may be chosen in twenty-eight exquisite colours. The Brushes are filled with best quality pure bristles and will give excellent service.
The 6-piece ERINOID TOILET BRUSH SET illustrated, is available in 28 beautiful colourings. **£3.17.6**

Also 4-piece ERINOID SHINGLE SETS including Hair Brush, Mirror, Cloth Brush and Comb. **£1.10.0**

Presentation Case 19/6
The above Set may be had with the backs lacquered at an additional cost of 30/-

Presentation Case 12/-
The Shingle Set may be had with the backs lacquered at an additional cost of 15/-

Separate Pieces are also available in the full size set :—
Mirror 16/- Hair Brush 20/- Cloth Brush 12/9 Hat Brush 8/9 Comb 2/6 Tray 9/6 Shoe Lift 3/6
Powder Bowl, 4½ ins. 7/6 Hair Tidy, 4½ ins. 7/6 Button Hook 1/9 Glove Stretcher 5/6
HARRODS LTD   *Telephone SLOane 1234*   LONDON SW1

△ Harrod's – Britain's most exclusive store – offers plastic as the height of fashion and good taste. Its light weight was a special selling point.

◁ Igor Sikorsky constructed the first American helicopter in 1939.

▷ In 1937, the Golden
Gate Bridge opened,
connecting San Francisco
with Oakland. At that
time, it had the longest
span in the world. The
bridge took five years to
complete.

◁ A family watches an experimental
television transmission in 1930 on
equipment devised by the Scottish
inventor John Logie Baird, who had
produced the first television picture
in 1925. By 1938, 20,000 television
sets were in service in New York
City.

▷ London's Battersea Power
Station, designed by Sir Giles G. Scott
and built between 1929 and 1935
was a potent symbol of the new
importance of electricity in industry
and in the home.

23

Radio

In 1930, 13,750,000 American households had radios, a figure that more than doubled by 1939. The number of licensed radio stations increased from 618 to 778 during the same period. Audience research indicated that the most popular radio programs were variety shows, dance music, and sports, that more women listened than men, more old than young, and that peak listening times were at midday and in the early evening.

Listeners could tune in to a wide range of commercial programs. Former vaudevillians like Eddie Cantor, George Burns, and Gracie Allen delighted radio audiences with their comedy routines. Music lovers could hear Arturo Toscanini conducting the NBC Symphony Orchestra and George Gershwin playing his own compositions. Crooners Rudy Vallee and Bing Crosby attracted many fans. During the daytime, radio stations scheduled continuing domestic dramas. These popular serials, sponsored by detergent manufacturers, gave the English language a new term – the "soap opera."

△ *Radio Pictorial* was one of a crop of specialist magazines aimed at the general listener as well as the technically-minded enthusiast. Notice the cover's emphasis on music. In 1990, Britain's biggest-selling magazine was still the *Radio Times*.

◁ Jack Benny's weekly show featured such regulars as Eddy "Rochester" Anderson, Mary Livingston, Don Wilson, Mel Blanc, and Dennis Day. Listeners enjoyed his famous "feud" with fellow comedian and personal friend Fred Allen.

◁ A French advertisement for radios emphasizes their technical features.

△ King Edward VIII broadcasts his abdication in 1936 by means of the radio.

△ Paul Robeson, the celebrated American baritone, poses in front of a typical 1930s radio. Music reached the largest audiences of anything broadcasting offered and, listening became a family event.

▷ The young Orson Welles's radio version of H. G. Wells's science-fiction fantasy *War of the Worlds* in October 1938 threw New Yorkers into such a panic that many fled the city from supposed Martian invaders.

The Stars

Many films were made to cash in on the popular appeal of a particular actor or actress, so that the actual plot was a secondary consideration providing it made the most of the talents of the leading players. Ordinary moviegoers confirmed the producers' insight when they habitually referred to a new film not by its title but as "a Ronald Colman" or "an Errol Flynn" film. Stars were news on and off the screen. The most successful could afford to live lavishly but it was risky to live scandalously, or, like Bette Davis, to try to resist the power of the studios by picking and choosing the parts that they wanted to play. From the studio's point of view stars were a major investment, to be kept constantly at work unless they lost their appeal and then were to be ruthlessly discarded.

Some stars, like platinum blonde Jean Harlow, enjoyed brief but brilliant fame. Others, like Charles Laughton or Katharine Hepburn, laid the foundations of long careers and enduring reputations. But it was the producers who controlled the purse strings.

△ Leslie Howard (1890–1943), born Leslie Stainer, specialized in the role of romantic and sensitive hero. He starred in *The Scarlet Pimpernel* (1934) and *Gone with the Wind* (1939).

◁ Shirley Temple in *Rebecca of Sunnybrook Farm* (1938). In *Bright Eyes* (1934) the foremost child star of the decade sang "The Good Ship Lollipop" and won an Academy Award.

◁ In *Mutiny on the Bounty* (1935), Charles Laughton played the tyrannous Captain Bligh while Clark Gable, "the King of Hollywood," was Fletcher Christian, the mutineers' tortured leader.

▽ Greta Garbo as "Queen Christina." Born Greta Louvisa Gustafsson in 1905, she dominated the 1930s in such films as *Anna Karenina* (1935) and *Ninotchka* (1939).

△ Marlene Dietrich, born Maria Magdalena von Losch, shot to fame in *The Blue Angel* (1930) and remained a screen legend.

The movies

In the 1930s, the "movies" became the "talkies." The addition of sound to pictures increased the importance of the script and the scriptwriter. Humor became less purely visual. The Marx Brothers, for example, combined traditional slapstick and stunts with a stream of wisecracks, double-talk and even musical gags. American slang, spoken on screen by gangsters, journalists or cowboys, spread throughout the English-speaking world.

Fashions and hairstyles were similarly influenced by the continually changing Hollywood modes. But if "the dream factory" offered glamour it also promoted morality.

From 1934 onwards, a detailed production code was strictly observed by the eight major studios that controlled 95 percent of American film output. On the silver screen, love always ended in marriage and crime was never allowed to pay. However, the weekly newsreel ensured that everyone saw a little of what was really going on in the world around them.

△ Stan Laurel and Oliver Hardy – clowns of genius. Their efforts to be stylish or ambitious invariably ended in disaster and destruction much to the enjoyment of their audiences.

▽ *Gone with the Wind* (1939) was Hollywood spectacle at its very best – big stars, big scenes and a big, big budget. The result was a resounding success on both sides of the Atlantic.

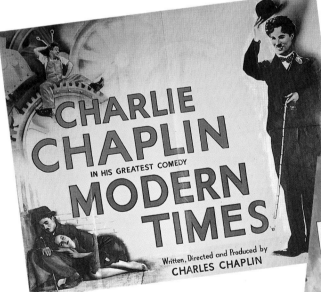

△ British born Charlie Chaplin, already a superstar by the 1930s, made a successful transition from silent to sound. *Modern Times* was his wry comment on the drawbacks of the machine age. Chaplin used a mixture of pathos and parody to represent the "little man's" view.

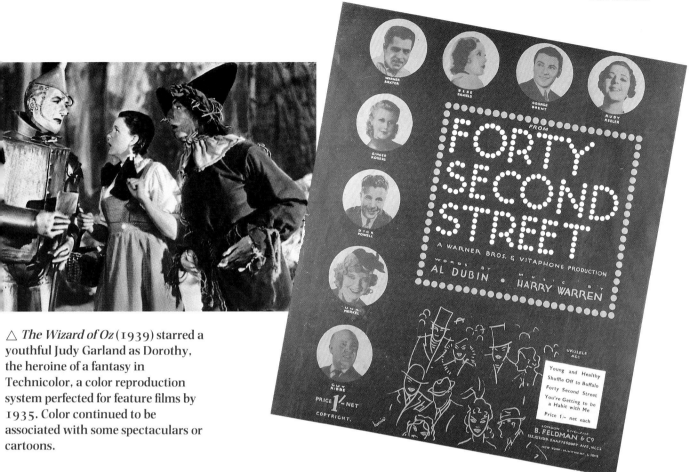

△ *The Wizard of Oz* (1939) starred a youthful Judy Garland as Dorothy, the heroine of a fantasy in Technicolor, a color reproduction system perfected for feature films by 1935. Color continued to be associated with some spectaculars or cartoons.

△ Sheet music for *42nd Street*, one of many dance spectaculars directed by Busby Berkeley. An ex-Army officer, he drilled mass-formations of chorus girls to perfection and made inventive use of unusual camera angles.

◁ *King Kong* (1933) made sensational use of special effects. The terrifying "monster" gorilla was in fact an articulated doll that measured less than two feet high.

Music and dance

During the 1930s, a new style of popular music, called "Swing," attracted a widespread and devoted following. Big bands, capable of filling vast dance halls with sound, were the order of the day. Their bandleaders – Harry James, Benny Goodman and the Dorsey Brothers – were idolized, while many of the singers remained almost anonymous by comparison. Instrumental soloists were an important feature of the bands.

Black music began to develop in many ways. Actress Josephine Baker emerged as an international star. Mahalia Jackson, grandmother of modern gospel music, made her first recording, as did the legendary Billie Holiday and Ella Fitzgerald.

The folk music of the American West received serious attention from Woody Guthrie who gathered together many of his songs while living as a tramp. Hollywood countered with Gene Autry ("The Singing Cowboy"). Important inventions included the electric guitar and organ.

△ "Fred and Ginger," the inspiration for a thousand light-footed fantasies. Fred Astaire and Ginger Rogers were not only brilliant dancers but also highly competent players of light comedy in a string of film hits.

◁ "We're in the Money!" proclaim the chorus of Busby Berkeley's lavish *Golddiggers of 1933* – an ironic refrain for an America deep in depression.

▷ A 1932 dance marathon for engaged couples. Contestants danced around the clock until they dropped out from sheer exhaustion. Survivors could win cash prizes and brief publicity.

▽ *Porgy and Bess,* George Gershwin's "folk opera," set among the poor black community of a fishing village in the South, opened in New York in 1935.

▷ "King of Swing" Benny Goodman (left) was the first bandleader to play jazz in Carnegie Hall.

Readers and writers

In the thirties, reading was a popular pastime. The public welcomed the arrival of such publishing innovations as paperback books and *Life* magazine. Americans bought one million copies of Margaret Mitchell's epic Civil War novel *Gone with the Wind* in just six months. Dashiell Hammett's detective stories, *The Thin Man* and *The Maltese Falcon,* were also best sellers. Film rights and best sellers made some authors quite wealthy while others depended on subsidies from the New Deal's Federal Writers Project.

Many literary works of this era went on to become classics. Among them was John Steinbeck's definitive novel about the Depression, *The Grapes of Wrath.* Outstanding dramatic plays included Thornton Wilder's tribute to small-town America, *Our Town;* Eugene O'Neill's modern adaption of a Greek tragedy, *Mourning Becomes Electra;* and Clifford Odets's boxing melodrama, *Golden Boy.* Poets Archibald MacLeish and Robert Frost each produced memorable volumes of verse.

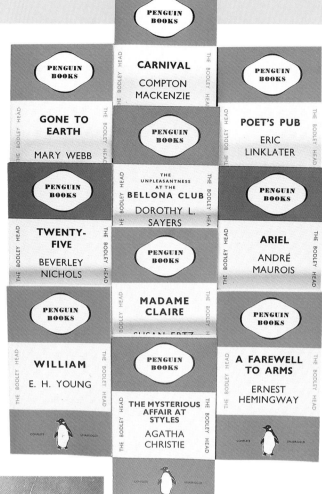

△ Penguin Books, launched in 1936, pioneered the "paperback revolution," publishing both "classics" and new works for less than the price of a movie ticket. In due course they were to influence not only leisure reading but education as well.

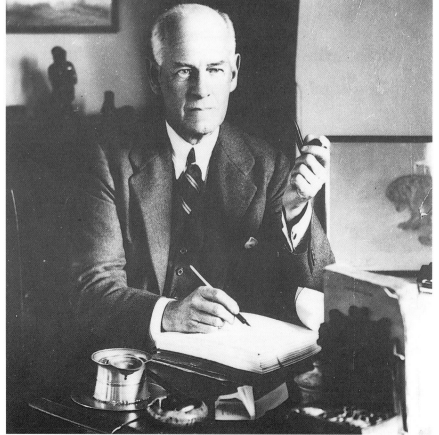

◁ British novelist John Galsworthy, whose immense *Forsyte Saga* novel series criticized the moral emptiness of the propertied classes which made up the majority of his readers. He won the Nobel Prize for Literature in 1932.

◁ H. G. Wells's futuristic *Things to Come* foretold of world war and the salvation of mankind. A. J. Cronin's *The Citadel* (center) chronicled a doctor's struggles against social injustice. John Steinbeck's *The Grapes of Wrath* (below left) exposed the plight of migrant farm workers. All three novels were made into successful films.

▽ P. G. Wodehouse ("Plum") won enduring popularity as the author of humourous stories featuring young Englishmen in wildly improbably situations. The most English of authors, whose characters inhabited a land of great country houses and eternal summers, Wodehouse himself spent most of his life abroad.

Fashion

In the the 1930s, a "smart appearance" was as much a matter of respectability as of fashion. Men were rarely seen outside the house without a jacket and hat. Even a working man would sport a muffler (scarf) and soft cloth cap. Women, likewise, wore hats and gloves on almost every occcasion and some people clearly distinguished between clothes for morning, afternoon and evening, as well as between town and country wear. One of the worst features of unemployment was the slide into shabbiness.

Fashion for women favored tailored, close-fitting clothes to give a slim, elegant line. Although chain stores made inexpensive, mass-produced clothes more widely available for both sexes, it was quite usual for middle-class men and women to have clothes handmade by a tailor or dressmaker. The sewing machine and hand-knitting enabled the less well-off to cater to their own individual tastes as well. Tennis, golf and holiday cruises inspired a gradual trend towards more casual clothes.

HIGH LIFE TAILOR

AUTOMNE-HIVER 1931

Extrait du catalogue de HIGH LIFE TAILOR, 112, rue de Richelieu et 12, rue Auber, Paris.

Pardessus droit, sur mesures.. **395 fr.** Manteau, entièrement doublé lighting. garni fourrure.

HIGH LIFE TAILOR envoie gracieusement son catalogue de luxe de costumes sur mesures, sans essayage contenant la manière de prendre soi-même ses mesures strictement exactes, à toute demande adressée 112, rue de Richelieu ou 12, rue Auber, Paris. (Aucune succursale en province ni à l'étranger, même s'intitulant HIGH LIFE TAILOR.)

A toute demande de l'étranger un mandat de frs : 5 devra être joint.

△ When the Prince of Wales wore a straw "boater," everybody wanted one.

▷ A Parisian tailor's catalog offers the high society look.

◁ An Italian advertisement for stockings. Legs demanded adornment and the new artificial fiber rayon offered a cheaper alternative to costly silk.

(Below left) Extravagant night attire fashions were inspired by Hollywood's "femmes fatales." With central heating still a rarity, most people settled for cozier and more practical alternatives.

▽ Developing a sun tan was a new idea and suggested the luxury of Mediterranean vacations and winter cruises.

Art and design

The 1930s' designers, adapting earlier trends to the new decade, sought to apply the principles of good design to objects of daily use. The emphasis was on "functionalism" (fitness for use) and an avoidance of unnecessary clutter or decoration for its own sake. Characteristics of this style could be seen as simple lines and economical use of space.

At the same time they also had to face the challenge of using new materials such as chrome, bakelite (an early form of plastic) or rayon, one of the first artificial fibers. They also had to design novel household appliances to fulfill the demand arising from the rapid spread of electricity into ordinary homes.

In Communist Russia and the Fascist states, designers and artists were often burdened with the need to show that their work portrayed and expressed approved political values. In Germany Hitler even organized an exhibition of "degenerate art" with which to underline the point.

△ In its stark simplicity, this steel chair sums up the design ideal of the 1930s, that of elegance and usefulness combined.

◁ The brightness and clean lines of the Hoover factory building in west London expressed the new face of smokeless industry based on electricity, another aspect of modernism.

BECK

◁ A stylized map of the London Underground railway system – a design "classic" that was still in use, little changed, over 50 years later.

▽ The Seven Deadly Sins by German expressionist artist Otto Dix (1891–1969) showed the darker fears of a troubled decade. Following Hitler's orders, Dix was jailed in 1939.

▽ In 1931, the Empire State Building opened its doors to the public. The steel-framed 102-story New York skyscraper took two years to complete. At a height of 381 m (1,250 ft), it was the world's tallest building for over 20 years.

Sports

Although the Depression decreased attendance, professional sports developed mass appeal during the 1930s. Thanks to radio broadcasts and movie newsreels, fans could enjoy the exploits of boxer Joe Louis, the "Bronx Bomber," or the antics of St. Louis Cardinal pitchers Daffy and Dizzy Dean without having to be there in person.

During the thirties, spectators who did attend sporting events witnessed a number of "firsts." Racetracks started to use electric totalizers to issue betting tickets and flash the odds on indicator boards.

The major leagues began to hold baseball games at night and initiated yearly all-star games. The Baseball Hall of Fame opened in Cooperstown, New York. The New York Yankees broke records by winning the World Series four times in succession. The National Football League inaugurated championship playoffs, while outstanding college players received the new Heisman Trophy. Professional golfers could also now compete in the Masters Tournament held at Augusta, Georgia.

BERLIN·1936
1-16 AUG.

OLYMPISCHE SPIELE

AUSKUNFTE UND WERBESCHRIFTEN DURCH ALLE REISE- UND VERKEHRSBÜROS

△ The 1936 Berlin Olympic Games were intended by Hitler to provide a convincing display of the racial superiority of "Aryan" athletes. This aim was decisively thwarted by a dazzling performance by American athlete Jesse Owens.

◁ American Jesse Owens set five world records in one afternoon in May 1935. At the 1936 Olympics, he won four gold medals for 100 meters, 200 meters, long jump and the 400 meter relay.

△ In 1938, New York Yankee Lou Gehrig set eight new major league records, but he retired in 1939, after 2,130 consecutive games, a victim of the disease that now bears his name.

△ Argentina equalize in the first ever World Cup final held at Montevideo in 1930. Home team Uruguay, however, went on to win 4-2. In 1934, Italy beat Czechoslovakia 2-1 and in 1938 defeated Hungary 4-2.

▷ American Helen Wills Moody, born in California in 1905, was known as "Little Miss Poker Face." She dominated the inter-war tennis scene, winning 19 major singles titles, including eight victories at Wimbledon.

Ideal homes

Low interest rates, the movement of people and the need to create jobs all helped to encourage large scale slum clearance and house-building programs in many countries. New homes incorporated many significant improvements such as more hygienic and better equipped kitchens and bathrooms and, more importantly, electricity to provide light and power for a wide range of household appliances. But, in 1939, 90 percent of British homes still relied on open fires as their main source of heating.

The United States was far more advanced in the use of major electrical appliances such as refrigerators and washing machines. Few European families, however, could aspire to more than a vacuum cleaner although many did possess an electric iron. Even as late as 1939, a third of homes in Britain still had no electricity.

Tastes in decor favored bold, geometric designs, "streamlined" shapes and pastel colors such as pale green or pink. Characteristic design features of the decade include highly polished wood, molded by steam into soft, curving lines complemented by shiny chrome and dark brown bakelite, a brittle plastic much used for handles and other small fittings.

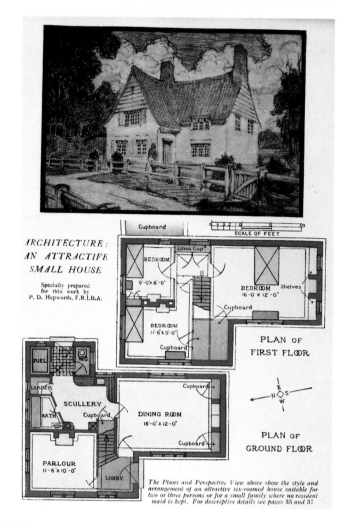

ARCHITECTURE: AN ATTRACTIVE SMALL HOUSE

Specially prepared for this work by P. D. Hepworth, F.R.I.B.A.

The Plans and Perspective View above show the style and arrangement of an attractive six-roomed house suitable for two or three persons or for a small family where no resident maid is kept. For descriptive details see pages 35 and 37

△ This model house still follows traditional cottage lines. It has no upstairs bathroom and incorporates such pre-electric features as a larder for food storage and an inside fuel store, for coal and wood.

KITCHEN
Modern Labour-Saving Kitchen For A Medium-Size House

The tiled recess contains an Aga heat-storage cooker burning coke or anthracite, and is flanked on the left by a refrigerator, and on the right by a cupboard for brooms. Further cupboard space is provided above. The two sinks are served by a single swivel tap with hot and cold turncocks. At the left of the sinks are a cupboard for pots and pans, and drawers for cooking cutlery and other implements. The facing wall, not shown, accommodates an electric washing-machine, a cupboard with ironing board and electric irons, a press for household linen, and a dry food store with slate shelves. The floor covering consists of green rubber squares, and rubber is used for covering the sink shelves and surrounds.

◁ This 1939 dream kitchen is centered on a solid fuel "Aga" stove, flanked by a broom closet (right) and a wall-mounted refrigerator. The floor and working surfaces are covered with rubber tiles and sheeting.

◁ This living room creates a bright and spacious feeling by avoiding clutter. Large numbers of ornaments, along with fussy patterns were thought "Victorian" and old-fashioned.

▽ A luxurious bathroom in Art Deco style echoes the legendary bathhouses of a Middle Eastern harem. But millions of people still had to be content with a portable tin tub in the kitchen, filled from kettles.

△ A page of electrical appliances from a store catalog features side- and standard-lamps but also shows flashlights, an iron and a hair dryer. A hair dryer would cost more than twice as much as the weekly unemployment allowance for a single person.

Growing up

Throughout the interwar years, there was a marked trend towards smaller families. The reasons were complex – a shortage of marriageable men after World War I, unemployment, the spread of birth control, later marriage and the desire to have fewer children so that each could be better cared for and educated. More and more children began to grow up in homes that were cleaner and less crowded, watched over by parents with more time to give them individual attention and affection. The trend was more clearly marked in middle-class than working-class homes.

The Depression took a toll on education. In 1933, it was estimated that 2,280,000 children were not going to school. Two thousand rural schools had closed down. A government report claimed that one third of the nation's schoolchildren were receiving an inadequate education. However, the illiteracy rate continued to drop reaching 4.2 percent at the end of the decade.

△ Board games became very popular as a cheap way of providing entertainment in the home for all the family.

◁ During the 1930s, actor Mickey Rooney made a memorable series of films idealizing adolescence. He portrayed the lovesick, bumbling teenager Andy Hardy, growing up in a small town.

▷ In Germany, the "Hitler Youth" was the only permitted organization for young people. It promoted physical toughness, comradeship, and a loyalty to Nazi ideals.

△ Comics were avidly read on both sides of the Atlantic, although the heroes and cartoon characters originated almost entirely from the United States. Comics also began to draw on the movies for their stories.

▷ Faced with the prospect of unemployment, many young men volunteered to join the Civilian Conservation Corps. Started by President Roosevelt in 1933, they worked outdoors on reforestation and construction projects. They received wages of $30 a month of which $22 was sent home.

Personalities of the 1930s

Astaire, Fred (1899-1987), elegant dancer, born Frederick Austerlitz, made many movie musicals with Ginger Rogers during the 1930s.

Chamberlain, (Arthur) Neville (1869–1940), British Prime Minister who supported the policy of appeasement and negotiated the Munich Pact of 1938.

Chiang Kai-Shek (1887–1975), Chinese General who seized control of the Chinese Nationalist Party (Kuomintang) and put down successive army revolts to become dictator of China. From 1937, he cooperated with the Communists to oppose Japanese invasion.

Disney, Walt (1901–66), American filmmaker whose cartoon creation Mickey Mouse became an international figure in the 1930s. Disney then moved on to full-length color cartoon features such as *Snow White* (1938) and *Pinocchio* (1939).

Earhart, Amelia (1897–1937), American aviator who was the first woman to fly solo across the Atlantic in 1932 and to fly alone from Hawaii to California in 1935. On a flight around the world, she disappeared over the Pacific Ocean and was never found.

Galsworthy, John (1867–1933), British novelist who sought to expose social changes and injustices.

Creator of *The Forsyte Saga*, he was awarded the Nobel Prize for Literature in 1932.

Garcia Lorca, Federico (1898–1936), renowned Spanish poet and playwright, he was shot by Nationalists at the outbreak of the Civil War.

Gershwin, George (1898–1937), versatile American composer who wrote popular songs, musical comedies, and serious orchestral pieces. His show *Of Thee I Sing* won the Pulitzer Prize in 1931. *Porgy and Bess,* his black folk opera, opened on Broadway in 1935.

Haile Selassie (1891–1975), crowned Emperor of Ethiopia in 1930, he tried to modernize his vast, impoverished country but was forced into exile (1936-41) by Italian invaders.

Harlow, Jean (1911–37), American film star whose sex appeal and gift for comedy brought her immense popularity before kidney failure brought untimely death.

Hitler, Adolf (1889–1945), megalomaniac dictator of Nazi Germany, called the *Führer* (leader). In the 1930s, he crushed all opposition to his rule and transformed Germany into a powerful war machine to support his aggressive foreign policy. After

gaining territorial concessions from weaker nations, he invaded Poland, an act that started World War II.

Louis, Joe (1914–81), the "Brown Bomber" who won the world heavyweight boxing title in 1937 and defended it 25 times to retire undefeated.

Moody, Helen Wills (1905–), American tennis superstar who, in 1938, won the Wimbledon women's singles title for a record eighth time.

Mosley, Sir Oswald (1896–1980), founder of the Fascist movement in Britain. He began his political life as a Conservative, then served as a Labor minister in 1929-30 before quitting to found the short-lived "New Party." His 1932 visit to Rome cast him under Mussolini's spell but, by 1934, his British Union of Fascists had swung towards Hitler and anti-Semitism. The Public Order Act of 1936, banning private armies and political uniforms, sent his movement into decline.

Mussolini, Benito (1883–1945), Fascist dictator of Italy, known as the *Duce* (leader). His imperialistic foreign policy resulted in the Italian conquest of Ethiopia in 1936 and the occupation of Albania in 1939. On the eve of World War II, he aligned his nation with Hitler's Germany, having formed the Rome-Berlin Axis in 1936.

Neville Chamberlain

Benito Mussolini

Jesse Owens

Orwell, George (1903–50), emerged as a major writer with the publication of *Down and Out in Paris and London* (1933), based on his own experiences of destitution. *Burmese Days* (1935), a criticism of British imperial rule, *The Road to Wigan Pier* (1937), an exposé of industrial depression and *Homage to Catalonia* (1938) about the Spanish Civil War, were likewise based on firsthand knowledge. He also wrote satirical novels such as *A Clergyman's Daughter* (1935), *Keep the Aspidistra Flying* (1936) and *Coming Up for Air* (1939).

Owens, Jesse (1913–80), American athlete who upset Hitler's claims of Aryan superiority by winning four gold medals at the 1936 Berlin Olympics.

Picasso, Pablo (1881–1973), gifted and prolific Spanish artist whose work is divided into overlapping periods based on his use of color and style. In the 1930s he worked on paintings and sculptures, but he also found time to illustrate more than 35 literary works. Loyal to the republican cause during the Spanish Civil War, Picasso completed his famous painting, *Guernica*, a passionate denunciation of Fascism and war, in 1937.

Pu-Yi, Henry (1906–67), reigned briefly as the last Manchu emperor of China (1908-12) before being appointed by the Japanese as Emperor K'ang Te of the puppet state of Manchukuo (1934-45).

Roosevelt, Franklin Delano (1882–1945), the only American president to be reelected three times. His "New Deal" policies fought economic depression by creating employment through major public works such as dams and reforestation projects, by payments to tide farmers over bad times and by new laws to support workers' rights. Through skillful use of radio, he used his "fireside chats" to bring himself closer to ordinary people than any previous president.

Simpson, Wallis Warfield (1896-1986), American-born wife of the Duke of Windsor, formerly King Edward VIII, who abdicated the British throne to marry her in 1937.

Smith, Bessie (1894–1937), American jazz singer and song-writer, known as the "Empress of the Blues," who recorded over 200 songs before being killed in a car crash.

Stalin, Josef (1879–1953), born Josef Vissarionovich Dzhugashvili. As general secretary of the Communist party in the 1930s, he used violence and terror to push through his policies of economic planning, industrialization, and collectivized agriculture in Russia. Opposed to Hitler, Stalin tried to form alliances with the European democracies. Rebuffed by the West, he signed a nonaggression pact with Nazi Germany in 1939.

Steinbeck, John (1902–68), American author known for his compassionate novels about the poor and dispossessed. His first commercial success, *Tortilla Flat* (1935), dealt with Mexican-Americans in Monterey, California. Steinbeck's novelette *Of Mice and Men* (1937) examined the strange bond between two migrant laborers. *The Grapes of Wrath* (1939), his Pulitzer prize winning work, drew attention to the plight of Dust Bowl farmers who migrated to California in search of work during the Depression.

Temple, Shirley (1928–), American child film superstar, who received a special Academy Award (Oscar) at the age of six. Her films include *Curly Top* (1935), *Heidi* (1937) and *Wee Willie Winkie* (1937). In adult life she entered politics and became a U.S. ambassador.

Wells, H. G. (1866–1946), English science-fiction novelist who also combined scientific interest with social concern. *The Shape of Things to Come* (1933) prophesied the terrible effects of aerial bombing in future wars and was soon made into a film.

Haile Selassie

John Steinbeck

Duchess of Windsor

1930s year by year

1930

- Britain, the United States, France, and Italy sign a naval disarmament treaty.
- The last Allied troops leave the Rhineland and the Saar.
- Coolidge Dam is dedicated.
- Grant Wood completes his painting "American Gothic."
- First sales of frozen food.
- Uruguay defeats Argentina 4–2 to win first soccer World cup.
- Planet Pluto discovered.
- Invention of perspex and photoflash bulb.
- Gandhi leads civil disobedience campaign against British rule in India.
- France begins construction of Maginot Line frontier defenses against Germany.
- Deaths of writers D. H. Lawrence, Roberts Bridges and Sir Arthur Conan Doyle.

1931

- National Government comes to power in Britain.
- German airship Graf Zeppelin flies around the world.
- J. G. Lansky detects stellar emissions coming from the Milky Way.
- The George Washington Bridge linking New York and New Jersey opens.
- Pearl Buck's first novel, *The Good Earth,* is published.
- Harold C. Urey discovers deuterium, popularly known as heavy water.
- Empire State Building completed in New York as world's tallest building.
- United States adopts "Star-Spangled Banner" as its national anthem.
- Walt Disney makes first color film, *Flowers and Trees.*
- Deaths of ballerina Anna Pavlova,

opera singer Dame Nellie Melba, novelist Arnold Bennett and inventor Thomas Edison.

1932

- King George V makes first royal Christmas radio broadcast.
- Franklin D. Roosevelt wins the United States presidential election.
- General Douglas MacArthur breaks up Bonus March on Washington, D.C.
- James Chadwick discovers the neutron.
- Ferde Grofe composes *The Grand Canyon Suite.*
- Amelia Earhart becomes the first woman to fly solo across the Atlantic.
- Vitamin D discovered.
- *Normandie,* world's largest liner, launched by France.
- Olympic Games held in Los Angeles.
- Salazar establishes Fascist regime in Portugal.
- Sir Thomas Beecham establishes London Philharmonic Orchestra.
- The Soviet Union begins second Five Year Plan for economic modernization.
- Cologne-Bonn autobahn opened.
- Japanese puppet state of Manchukuo set up in Manchuria.
- Son of Charles Lindbergh kidnapped and found murdered.

1933

- Hitler becomes Chancellor of Germany, followed by Reichstag fire and persecution of German Jews.
- Japan withdraws from the League of Nations.
- H. G. Wells's *The Shape of Things to Come* is published.
- The United States goes off the gold standard.
- Vitamin C is synthesized.
- Franklin Delano Roosevelt

inaugurates "New Deal" economic recovery policies in the United States.
- Prohibition of alcohol repealed in America.
- Deaths of former U.S. President Calvin Coolidge and British novelist John Galsworthy.

1934

- "Stavisky" riots in France against government corruption.
- Austrian Chancellor Dollfuss assassinated.
- King Alexander of Yugoslavia assassinated.
- Luxury liner *S. S. Queen Mary* launched in the United Kingdom.
- Chinese Communist leader Mao Tse Tung begins 6,000 miles "Long March".
- The Soviet Union joins the League of Nations.
- Ruth Benedict's *Patterns of Culture* is published.
- German President von Hindenburg dies and Adolf Hitler declares himself "Der Führer."
- Deaths of composers Sir Edward Elgar, Gustav Holst and Frederick Delius and of scientist Marie Curie.

1935

- The Social Security Act becomes law in the United States.
- George Gershwin's folk opera *Porgy and Bess* opens.
- Canada pioneers first broadcast quiz show.
- Alcoholics Anonymous is organized in New York City.
- Italy invades Abyssinia (Ethiopia).
- Persia changes its name to Iran.
- Pan-American Airways starts trans-Pacific service.
- American athlete Jesse Owens sets six world athletic records in one hour.
- Turkey requires all citizens to take

a surname.

- Germany re-introduces compulsory military service.
- Lower Zambesi Railway Bridge, the longest in the world, opened to traffic.
- Death of war hero and writer T. E. Lawrence ("Lawrence of Arabia"), and comedian Will Rogers.

1936

- Edward VIII becomes King and abdicates in favor of his brother, the Duke of York.
- Outbreak of civil war in Spain.
- Unopposed German troops reoccupy Rhineland in violation of 1919 Treaty of Versailles.
- Olympic Games staged in Berlin.
- Hitler and Mussolini proclaim the Rome-Berlin Axis.
- Henry Luce begins to publish *Life* magazine.
- Franklin D. Roosevelt is elected to a second term as President of the United States.
- Publication of Margaret Mitchell's blockbuster novel *Gone With the Wind.*
- Athlete Jesse Owens wins four gold medals at the Olympic Games in Berlin.
- John Maynard Keynes' "General Theory of Employment, Interest and Money" argues that governments can avoid economic depressions.

1937

- German airship *Hindenburg* crashes killing 34 people.
- German Condor Legion bombers destroy Spanish town of Guernica.
- Marco Polo Bridge incident prompts Japanese invasion of China.
- Roosevelt signs Neutrality Act to keep America out of a European war.
- Aviator Amelia Earhart

disappears over the Pacific Ocean while on an around-the-world flight.
- Insulin used to control diabetes.
- Jet engine and nylon stockings invented.
- The first transcontinental radio program is broadcast in the United States.
- Japanese planes sink U.S. gunboat Panay in Chinese waters.
- Neville Chamberlain becomes British prime minister and the policy of appeasement begins.

1938

- Germany annexes Austria.
- Walter Gropius and Marcel Breuer complete the Haggerty House, their first work in the United States.
- Douglas G. "Wrong-Way" Corrigan flies to Ireland insisting he was headed for California.
- Orson Welles causes a panic with his broadcast of H. G. Wells's *War of the Worlds.*
- The ballpoint pen is invented.
- Vitamin E is identified.
- Munich crisis ends in apparent resolution of the position of Sudeten Germans at the expense of Czechoslovak sovereignty.
- Nylon toothbrush introduced.
- First xerox photocopy made.
- Walt Disney releases first feature-length cartoon *Snow White and the Seven Dwarfs.*

1939

- Germany conquers Poland and divides its territory with the Soviet Union.
- Britain and France declare war on Germany.
- Russia invades Finland.
- DDT invented.
- Italy invades Albania.
- King George VI and Queen

Elizabeth become the first British sovereigns to visit the United States.
- FM radio transmission is developed.
- John Steinbeck's *The Grapes of Wrath* is published.
- Igor Sikorsky constructs the first helicopter.
- Nuclear fission discovered.
- World fair in New York

Index

48

PRINTED IN BELGIUM BY
proost
INTERNATIONAL BOOK PRODUCTION